CERTIFICATE OF APPRECIATION

Awarded To

Gary, my BT. I love you. Without you,
I would be running around in circles.

www.mascotbooks.com

I Teach, Therefore I Wine

For more information, please contact:

Mascot Books
620 Herndon Parkway, Suite 320
Herndon, VA 20170
info@mascotbooks.com

Library of Congress Control Number: 2018902665

CPSIA Code: PRTWP0318A
ISBN-13: 978-1-68401-644-0

Printed in Malaysia

I TEACH, THEREFORE I ~~WHINE~~

WINE

Christina
Hammons

Contents

A Pour Decision

You absolutely love your job, regardless of your constant moaning and groaning about it. You know that only a select few can appreciate all that goes into teaching, and even fewer can recognize the sacrifices you make to carry out the mission well. You also love wine. You know that some of your favorite memories are those spent storytelling with friends over a glass or two. During one of those visits, you pour out a ridiculous idea, like a blind tasting, about how stories from the frontlines should be paired with a particular wine. Examples start to spill out, and laughter erupts. You let the idea age a bit. You bring it up in another setting, another time, and again the energy changes in the room, and everyone comes alive with stories to wine about. You decide to harvest your idea. You press on, crushing out the details and letting the concepts ferment. You seek assistance for clarification from trusted sources, and after the manuscript ages for some time, it's bottled and made available for consumption. Your only remaining desire is that those sampling I Teach, Therefore I Wine find as much joy in its pages as you did in its vinification.

PAIRED WITH
Manuscript
Manuscript Cellars Winery

WINE

NOUN

1. an alcoholic drink made from fermented grape juice

ex.: She opened a bottle of red wine.

VERB

1. to entertain someone by offering them a drink and a meal

ex.: We wined and dined her.

Welcomes you after a long day

Invites you to rest and relax

Never judges or blames you

Encourages you to press forward

KINDRED SPIRITS

It is erroneous to suggest when people consider teachers they immediately think of children. It really is no secret that teachers have an intimate, up close, and personal relationship with fermented grapes. The two really are kindred spirits. As an educator myself, I have been researching this phenomenon for over a decade and can concur it is in fact true. Merchandise across the globe supports my research: shirts, hats, mugs, wine glasses all maintain my theory that teachers and wine are, undoubtedly, partners in education. As with any and all things, there is a gamut of passion for both. In education you have those who live and breathe teaching while others are counting down the days to retirement. In regard to wine, you have those who may savor the earthy blends of plum, noticing the subtle hint of blueberry pie. They experience the journey. Others believe in the adage "Love the wine you're with." They delight simply in the destination.

Teachers fall somewhere in the middle of that spectrum. Although we can appreciate the finer wines, we tend to judge a book by its cover, or in this case a wine by its label. Thus bringing us to the treasure you now have at your fingertips. Wine is paired with food to accentuate sweetness, balance tartness, and enhance the overall dining experience. Food is not the only thing that needs a little balance. Spend a day in the life of an educator and see if that experience doesn't have you knocking on the nearest wine cellar door. I can't fathom a situation a teacher might encounter that wouldn't be enhanced with a glass of wine at the end of the day. For those of you in doubt, please, read on. For those of you already in the know, I support your consumption habits with no judgment. So, without further ado, pour a glass of your favorite vino, swirl, sniff, and sip as you relish—and perhaps relate—to the tips and tales set forth in these pages.

Cheers!

IF TEACHING WERE A FINE WINE

Wine descriptions really are works of art. The figurative language and imagery used to articulate a particular wine is quite impressive and should be marveled. Seriously, when I see a bottle of wine and read its label, I see a lesson plan in the making. Imagine using wine labels for a unit of poetry, for instance. Although the material may not be the most developmentally appropriate, the objectives that could be covered are endless. Concepts from analyzing metaphors to recognizing other various literary elements such as foreshadowing and symbolism could all be mastered with just a few bottles of wine. It's something to consider. Yet, I've digressed. Regardless of the level of differentiation: bottom shelf, middle shelf, top shelf, all wines sound incredibly enticing, tantalizing, and exotic. It really makes me wonder what it might sound like if teaching were a fine wine…

Powerful and complex. A bold profession with earthy aromas of youth with a hint of graphite. Inviting nuances of 2 percent strawberry milk. A structured field combined with friendly experiences mingled with dense occurrences. High acidity at times, yet overall intellectually satisfying.

Sign me up, please! Now that I think about it, college made teaching sound a lot like that. Well, that's one label that didn't quite deliver its promise!

RED, WHITE, AND BLUSH

Most educators start their day with a cup of coffee and end it with a glass of wine. That has already been established. So the only real question that remains is whether it's a red, white, or blush night. It's not as simple as it may sound. There are many elements that must be taken into account when selecting a wine. It really is a situational decision that takes great care and consideration. Wine may improve with age, but any mood will improve with wine.

There are moments in a day that have you seeing **RED**. Red moments, similar to wines containing increased levels of intensity, can result in higher blood pressure and a lingering headache by the end of the day. They are exasperating, maddening experiences that send you to the dark side. Those are the incidents when your mind suggests one response, yet your body responsibly carries out something a little more appropriate. At least, we hope the body is a bit less impulsive than the mind. If not, those are nights a glass may turn into a bottle. Maddening moments are best extinguished when paired with a red wine.

Then there are moments you see a WHITE light at the end of a very dank and dreary tunnel. Those are the favorite moments of all educators. They're rewarding moments when hard work and dedication has paid off. They remind us why we chose the profession, that we really do adore children, and that there is hope for our future. Because white wine has a timeless feel to it with a deep yellow hue, holding a glass of it is like holding a Golden Globe Award. It is a true honor, and even better, it's perfectly acceptable to drink white wine after Labor Day. Pairing a glass of white wine with a moment that inspires, affirms, and rejuvenates a teaching spirit is exhilarating.

Moments that make you BLUSH might just be the toughest grape to swallow. Those are moments the unthinkable has occurred, and although you'd rather hide and watch, you are instead front and center for what is nothing less than pure unadulterated embarrassment. Your mind is asking "Did that just happen?" while your face betrays you and turns the color of a fruity rosé blend. It only makes sense to pair your humiliation with a blush wine.

To the untrained it may seem cumbersome to successfully pair an occasion with an appropriate wine. Fret no further. Uncork and relax because the scenarios and tales you are about to sample are guides that will fast-track you on your passage from novice to master wine connoisseur and student teacher to teacher retiree.

MOMENTS THAT HAVE
YOU SEEING RED

SERVING TIME

States and districts require continuing education hours for educators to ensure they remain lifelong learners. You are an advocate for professional development, although you rarely leave a workshop with feelings of fulfillment. You believe in the significance of keeping with educational trends, assuming they actually nurture child development, but more importantly you believe in adding to personal schema and growing as an educator. The moment you quit learning, you stop knowing, and knowledge really is power. However, you involuntarily find yourself trapped in a workshop that drags on for hours, rendering you nothing more than a headache. You feel imprisoned, and that makes you dark and bitter. No doubt there is one attendee that is convinced their ideas are all intoxicating, leaving you with the desire to put a cork in them. And this particular presenter made it clear from the start there will be no early release for good behavior.

Paired with

THE PRISONER
Red Blend

www.theprisonerwinecompany.com

BLANKET E-MAIL

You manage to find time to actually sit down at your desk and catch up on e-mails. You have what seems to be a billion waiting in your inbox. At the top of the unread mail you notice one marked urgent from your principal. You also quickly recognize that it is addressed to the entire staff. You begin reading it, a lengthy e-mail that goes into great detail about violations against staff handbook expectations. You immediately begin to self evaluate, first questioning your wardrobe. Are you breaking dress code? You then think back to the morning, when you arrived. Were you on time? You go back in time to the day before. Did you leave before your contract hours were up? You come to the conclusion that you are in the clear, and you speculate who might be the guilty party that initiated the scathing e-mail from administration. You think you have a pretty good idea to whom the e-mail is directed, but the truth is you have no clue the intended audience because the e-mail, although detailed in its complaint, is void of any indication of the true violators. You feel bold and do the one thing that demonstrates some semblance of power and control: you click "delete."

Paired with

CRYPTIC
Red

WINDBAG

OCCASION

How it happened, you'll never know, but you are on the committee led by none other than Ms. Hard-to-Get-Along-With. Your teammates giggle and heckle you as you make your way to the first scheduled "meeting of the minds," where ideas will be shared and decisions will be made before the committee announces the new implementations to the faculty. You do your best to avoid eye contact, mind your manners, and mind your business, all the while maintaining a professional appearance throughout the meeting. Every idea is quickly shot down, and every solution is deemed unacceptable. You wonder how this person was ever selected for a leadership position. Your attempt to fly below the radar and keep quiet only draws more attention to yourself since you tend to be a little more outspoken and resourceful in these types of settings. You realize your name has been called, and you look up to find yourself in you-know-who's line of vision. The question is posed, "You've been mighty quiet. Do you have anything you wish to add to our discussion?" Only two words come to mind. Rather than share it with the group, you reconcile that some things are best left unspoken.

Paired with

SASSY BITCH
Pinot Noir

www.sassybitchwines.com

OVER-COMMUNICATOR

You are taking care of odds and ends during your conference time. For once it is not being utilized for another meeting that will render a mood swing and ultimately lead to absolutely nowhere. You head to the teachers' work room to make a few copies and check your box for anything that needs immediate attention. You round the corner and see the one person you have deemed to be the "over-communicator" standing between where you are and where you need to be. You recall the last few times you engaged in a conversation with them. You know all about their personal life, health concerns, and family dysfunctions. You flashback to just how close communications with this individual can become since their personal space requires significantly less room than yours. You silently wonder how many glasses of wine it would take to actually enjoy being in the same vicinity as them. They see you about the same time you see them. You have no other choice but to smile, wave real big, and prepare yourself to, yet again, be shocked at what some people are willing to share.

Paired with

UNCENSORED
Red Blend

www.uncensoredwine.com

INSIDE RECESS

The meteorologist predicted the rain should hold off until late afternoon. You welcome the rain. You recognize the need for rain. You find great pleasure in the sound of the rain hitting the rooftop. You often look forward to the rain, as long as it is after recess. You are lining your students up and helping them file out onto the playground. You hear a rumble, and the other teachers look at you with utter fear in their eyes. Before they can speak you shout out, "That was the dumpster pickup truck!" You hear the rumble again. You remind everyone that there are two dumpsters on site. When the third rumble makes it clear that you are in fact hearing thunder, you look up into the sky and mentally wail, "Why!?" You have no other options. Recess will be inside. You spend the longest thirty minutes of your life, in the smallest confined area possible, with twice as many students that have no concept of "inside voices." You find a focal point in the room that allows for peripheral vision to ensure you are keeping an eye on everyone, and you wait for time to pass. It's as if you are watching paint dry—at a rock concert. As you are mentally drafting hate mail to the meteorologist, you promise that the next time you are required to monitor inside recess, the students will be watching a movie.

Paired with

FREAKSHOW
Red Blend

MOMENTS YOU SEE A WHITE LIGHT AT THE END OF THE TUNNEL

OCCASION

It is the last day of school for teachers. Students were sent home packing just days earlier, and you have been making progress on your end-of-year checklist by finalizing paperwork, cleaning out cabinets, and disposing of, from the desk of one of your most memorable students, what started weeks ago as a snack that can only be described now as a science experiment. You realize the last thing on your list is to turn in your badge and keys until the next school year. June, July, and August are moments away. You make the final walk down the hall to the front office, wishing everyone along the way an incredible summer and reveling in the knowledge that you will be kicking off your summer gazing at sparkling water while sipping a beverage rich in fruit flavors. For a moment you think you actually hear the waves crashing against the shore and taste the hint of citrus on your lips. You take a deep breath and relax for the first time in months because everyone knows life is better at the beach.

Paired with

BAREFOOT

Pinot Grigio

WELCOME TO MY WORLD

Whether it's winter break, spring break, or summer vacation, you are on an extended time-off from school. You have enjoyed yet another relaxing day doing only the things you wish to do rather than anything you have to do. You take a few minutes to check out social media. You smile to yourself when you see your fellow educators posting pictures of their day trips, staycations, or elaborate getaways. You know that those moments are all well deserved. You then come to a post by a parent of a well-known spirited student at your school. Although this special student is not in your class, you recall the times other parents suggested that there were so many behavior concerns with their child because you simply had low tolerance. You totally relate and sympathize with the teacher who was gifted this particular student for the school year. You then notice the post is a picture of a bottle of wine with the caption, "Counting the days until school is back in session!" You do a mental calculation yourself and celebrate the minutes you have left before welcoming back your class after the break. You cannot help but think to yourself, "Welcome to my world," as you tuck your device away and carry on with your rest and relaxation.

Paired with

BLISS

Chardonnay

www.blissvineyard.com

MOM

You adore your students, and they love you. Well, most of them love you. There is always at least one cherub with whom, no matter how hard you try, you struggle to make a personal connection. They hate school and remind you of their disdain often. Learning is a waste of time in their eyes. Following directions is a joke and something to avoid at all costs. This does not deter you. Your effort to learn all you can about this student has armed you with the information to break through their force field, allowing you to build a relationship with them. You know about their family, their extracurricular activities, and all of their strengths. You engage in conversations with them often to remind them that you do care and that they are important and have so much to offer the world. They continue to push you away and keep their distance. You are working with a small group of students as you notice One-Who-Hates-Everything approach holding the daily assignment and looking a bit confused. Before realizing what has happened, "Hey, Mom," tumbles right out of their mouth, and their face morphs into fear, embarrassment, and panic within seconds. You don't miss a beat as you reassure them that type of thing happens all the time, and you help them with their question right away. They thank you as they walk back to their desk, and your heart smiles and emanates pure happiness for the rest of the class period.

Paired with

PROJECT HAPPINESS
Chardonnay

www.oreanawinery.com

AH-HA

The end of a unit is right around the corner, and you have been beating your head against the wall trying to make sure every student is prepared to move onto the next concept. You have used every tool you have in your figurative tool box to teach the skill as many ways as you know possible. You are working with a student one-on-one before school because you believe the individual time will be just what it takes to help them meet success. You feel that you are losing the battle, so you pull out all the stops, and with great determination you start from the beginning. You reteach the very first strategy you used when introducing the concept to the class. Once you finish your spiel you say, "Now, tell me what that means to you." It's like a light turns on. Your student looks at you and grins as they reiterate the lesson. Without a doubt they understand what you have been working so hard to teach over the last several weeks. You high-five them and celebrate their success and hard work. Sip, Sip, Hooray! It's now on to the next concept.

Paired with

ONE HOPE
California Chardonnay

www.onehopewine.com

OCCASION

The last of the laundry has been folded. The floors are spotless after they were swept and mopped. Every inch of your house sparkles. You take one last glance at your closet that you've finally reorganized. You ask everyone in your home if they need your help with anything they're working on. You realize the answer is simply, "No." Why? Because you have managed to tackle every outstanding task that you have put off with the exception of one: grading your mammoth stack of papers. As you stare at it you are reminded of the Leaning Tower of Pisa. You have practiced avoidance long enough. You sit down with your giant tote bag of schoolwork that you carry to and from school every day regardless of whether or not you open it and your little bag of grading pens—you have one of every color because of your irrational fascination with school supplies—and you dive in, not coming up for air for about three hours. You score your last paper and for good measure draw a circle around the grade, adding a little swirl at the top. You gather up every last paper and shove them back into the tote. You tuck your pens away until they are needed again. You have never felt freer and you want to celebrate!

Paired with

LIBERATED
Sauvignon Blanc

MOMENTS THAT MAKE
YOU BLUSH

SPLIT DECISION

It is well into the first semester of the school year. Winter break is right around the corner, and you have been storing up fat for the season. Long gone are the days of prepping healthy meals ready to go. Nope. You've been living on school food, vending machines, and eating out to avoid cooking at home. You've been devouring your feelings for months. With great effort earlier in the day, you squeezed yourself into your favorite pair of jeans. You acknowledged at the time they looked a little worn, tattered, and rather thin. You, nonetheless, convinced yourself that look was trending and reminded yourself that denim was a fabric to be reckoned with. Besides, there was no way were you going to miss out on wearing jeans to work! You bend over to pick up material you will be using for your next lesson, and you not only hear the rip, you also feel the breeze. Holy cow (no pun intended), you just ripped your pants. You have a split decision to make. Fight-or-flight adrenaline kicks in. You can flee the scene—damned be the consequences—or you can grab your jacket off the back of your chair, wrap it around your waist, and teach on promising yourself to start that liquid diet as soon as you get home!

Paired with

FAT ASS STRAWBERRY FIELDS
Rosé

www.fatasswine.com

OCCASION

You are traveling with your class, using great effort to keep them calm, cool, and collected in the hallway. Because you have a chatty group, keeping them quiet has proven to be a rather difficult task. You've utilized all of your non-verbal classroom management strategies to no avail. It's time to move onto verbal cues. You make eye contact with one of your sweetest students who always chooses to follow directions the first time they are given, and you acknowledge what a fantastic job they are doing respecting all of the working classrooms you pass by on your journey to the cafeteria. That verbal tactic does not work. In fact, the majority of your class is oblivious to the praise you just awarded. The girls are giggling even louder, and the boys are jumping to see if they can hit the decorations hanging from the ceiling. You have lost your patience. You turn to face the mob that is your class, and from deep down, somewhere dark within, you string together a series of consequences they will face if they do not settle immediately. The class instantly responds. You feel like you have tamed the dragon, so you turn to continue to the lunchroom, only to find yourself face to face with your principal, who is in the middle of a school tour with a family looking to enroll their child. You haven't seen your principal in days, and all you can think is, "Why now?" You smile, hope they don't notice the deep shade of pink your face is flaunting, wish them all well, and make way to deposit your students in the cafeteria as if nothing ever happened.

Paired with

IMPATIENCE
Côtes de Provence

ROLL WITH IT

OCCASION

Your class has just transitioned to the next assignment. The room has gone from organized chaos, where students were actively engaged in groups and a lesson that made them love learning, to solemn and serious as they begin working on an independent assignment that is certain to render evidence that they have mastered the curriculum concepts. You head over to your desk to review your lesson plans and make sure you are keeping to your schedule. A wave of exhaustion hits, and you take advantage of the moment and steal the opportunity to sit down briefly. As you approach your chair you quickly realize you have misjudged your position. You tap the edge of your seat at just the right angle to push the rolling chair out from under you. Although time seems to have reverted to slow motion, you know it is only a millisecond after your ass hits the ground that you are back on your feet with hands in the air as if you just dismounted off the uneven bars at the Summer Olympics. Your class is jolted from their studies by the racket and look at one another to try and make sense of what just occurred. You admit nothing and instruct everyone to get back to work. You fan your face because the temperature in the room suddenly shot up to 100 degrees. You make like the chair and roll with it, accepting that your crack at proving Newton's laws of motion is guaranteed to leave a rosy mark.

Paired with

ACROBAT
Rosé of Pinot Noir

WHO DEALT IT

OCCASION

It's one of your favorite times of the day. You have your class gathered around you for story time. You believe that no matter the age, students should have the opportunity built into their day to enjoy listening to a good story. You've researched the benefits of reading aloud to children of all ages and can easily corroborate that this time is well utilized and should be treasured. Everyone is excited because the chapter ended with a cliffhanger the day before. Your class respects this time, so all ears are eager to listen, and voices are muted. In the silence you can hear a pin drop. Unfortunately it's not a pin that you hear; it sounds more like a duck's quack. The order that once was your class has erupted into pandemonium. Accusations are unleashed, and denials immediately get underway. No longer is the class a tight-knit group of eager readers. They are scattering to evade the lingering evidence that someone just passed gas and roses were the last thing on anyone's mind. It takes some time, yet you manage to corral everyone back together and remind them that what just occurred is perfectly natural and everyone does it. You use the story to divert and redirect your students. No one confesses to being the offender, although you know exactly who is responsible for the recent mayhem. Yep, you will be taking that information to the grave.

Paired with

DECOY
Rosé

www.decoywines.com

HOLD YOUR BALLS

You blow your whistle to signal that recess is over. Waves of children scurry to line up and prepare to reenter the building and carry on with the rest of their afternoon. Equipment has been collected, and a few students help put all the gear away. You do everything in your power to settle the crowd because there is no way you can enter the building in the current state of unruliness. After several attempts you finally have what appears to be a composed group. That is, with the exception of the equipment helpers who continue to bounce the basketballs. You are weathered from the extreme temperatures and frazzled from all the commotion. You want a moment of peace, so you decide to put an end to the noise from the children still playing with the equipment. In your most assertive voice you command, "Hold your balls!" Well, so much for order and harmony, because everyone ruptures into fits of laughter. Your fellow teaching comrades can't even maintain composure. You find yourself back at square one. You blow your whistle to signal that recess is over, again. Although the tension in your shoulders is intensifying, you are not one to complain; you prefer to wine. And wine you shall do as soon as you get home.

Paired with

TENSHEN
Rosé

www.tenshenwines.com

TRUE TALES TO WINE ABOUT

ACKNOWLEDGE AND MOVE ON

BY CAN I. GETANAMEN

I make it a point to greet my students at the door every morning. It's an excellent way for me to gauge their moods, but mostly I just want to welcome them and let them know that I'm excited about seeing them. It's also a great time to collaborate with neighboring teachers. I had one student who was all about the shock factor. He would go to great lengths to throw me off my game in hopes to surprise or distress me. After unpacking and opting to not settle into the class, he sought me out at the door. He then proceeded to shake his entire body, flail his arms, throw his head back as he rolled his eyes, all the while asking me if his actions made him look possessed. I responded with a deadpan expression and, "No, it makes you look like you are not following directions. Now it's time to get back to work." I acknowledged and moved on. My fellow teachers couldn't quite hold it together. Once the student headed back into the classroom, they lost it right there in the hallway!

" Teaching is like trying to hold fifty corks underwater at the same time. "

SHOW AND SHARE

BY AW K. WARD

I had "show and share" Fridays my first year of teaching. One boy couldn't wait to show and share something really cool. He explained that his mom had been to New Orleans for the weekend and brought back a "toy" in her suitcase. He had found it and thought it would be perfect to bring to school to share with the class. He then pulls out a fake hand and turns the switch to show how it vibrates while the middle finger rotates. Before he handed it to the first child in the circle I jumped up to grab it and put it away. I quickly asked, "Who would like to share next?"

"Today's forecast is 99% chance of wine."

THIS CAN'T BE LEGAL

BY HOPE NO ONESAW

It was nearing the last day of school, and students were bringing in sweet cards and generous gifts. It's always a bittersweet time of year for me because part of me is so excited to be able to spend the summer hours with my personal family and children, yet I get a little weepy thinking that our class traditions and memory-making moments will be a thing of the past. It was a little before the morning bell rang, and a student walked up to me with a big smile and a summer beach-style bag filled with goodies. I read the heartfelt card and started digging into the bag so the student could see just how excited I was about their gift. Luckily the bag was deep because as soon as I removed the tissue paper I was faced with multiple bottles of alcohol. My face got hot, and I panicked. All I could think was, "I'm going to get fired!" I faked a little emergency and told the student I couldn't wait to explore what else was in the bag once I got home. I gave them a big hug and tucked the gift behind my desk. It was one of the longest days of the school year. As soon as I got home I opened up that gift bag along with one of its contents!

"Keep your apples; I'd rather have wine."

NAPTIME

BY G. STRING

I was teaching pre-school, and the class was preparing for naptime. It was standard practice to lay out all of our mats and then each student would cover their nap pad with a mat sheet they brought from home. One student was shaking out his mat cover to place it over his nap pad when all of a sudden a lady's thong flew out of the sheet. When I say thong, I am not referring to a flip-flop. I remember standing there frozen in place, asking myself if I really just witnessed a pair of panties that looked like a slingshot fall out of that child's sheet. I quickly recovered and told the little boy, "Grab those up, put them in your bag, and take them home." That incident gave the saying "Don't get your panties in a wad" a whole new meaning.

"Sometimes wine is

just necessary."

CAT FOOD IS FOR CATS

BY M. E. OW

Notes from parents can be varied. They can be informative, questioning, happy, angry, thankful...you never know what you'll read. This is perhaps my all-time most memorable note that I received the first week of school during one of my years teaching fourth grade. It went something like this:

Dear Mrs. Ow,

Samantha brought to my attention that a girl in her class, Julie, got her to eat dry cat food at lunch yesterday. If Julie wants to bring cat food in her lunch and eat it, that is her business, but she may not give Samantha cat food to eat. She said she ate several pieces and then had a stomach ache.

Shortly after reading the note and speaking to Samantha to confirm that this all happened, I visited with Julie. I remember saying, "Cat food is for cats. Humans eat people food. You may not bring cat food to school in your lunch kit." Sometimes words come out of our mouths that we never think we'll have to say! The lunchroom was heavily monitored the next few days, with no signs of cat food at our table.

" Coffee keeps us busy until it's acceptable to drink wine."

SCALES

BY REP TILE

Once during a test, a student walked up to me and showed me his hand and asked with a concerned look on his face, "Do you see it? I'm changing." I replied, "Do I see what?" "I'm changing into a reptile. Can you see the scales and the skin changing?" he asked again. "No, honey, I can't see it yet. You don't have time to change into a reptile; you have to finish your test." Of course, I'm thinking he wanted out of taking his test, so I say, "Why don't you go finish your test, and then you can change into a reptile." He was satisfied with that response and completed his test, never to return asking about his reptilian skin again.

"I only drink wine when I'm alone or with someone."

A LITTLE PEE NEVER HURT ANYONE

BY DID U. SAYPEE

A sweet student brought his weekly folder back to school, very pleased that he had found it. It had been MIA for about a week. As he handed it to me, with a proud smile he said, "Mrs. Saypee, here's my Tuesday folder. Chuey peed on it, but don't worry. My mom cleaned it off."

"Wine may not solve your problems, but neither will milk or water."

HAPPY TEARS

BY I. MADE ADIFFERENCE

As an administrator in an elementary school, I can spend years working with a student and their behaviors. One of the most fulfilling days I've had in education was when a fifth grader cried in my office the last day of school and told me he was sad to leave for middle school because I was the only person who ever believed in him for such a long period of time. I cried too.

" I never wine when

I'm with you. "

PARDON MY GRAPE JUICE

BY SIP N. GRADE

I had committed to getting all of my piles of papers graded over the weekend. Mission accomplished! I was passing back all of the assignments the following Monday morning. Students, as usual, were either celebrating with "Oh Yeah!" or "Another 100%!" while others were sneaking their papers into the back of their folders in hopes that their peers would not see the scores at the top. One student tapped me on the shoulder, and when I turned around he was holding his poetry assignment and pointing to a purple stain on it. He asked, "What is this?" I quickly responded, "Oh honey, that is grape juice. I'm sorry. I must have spilled a little when I was grading your paper." I congratulated him on his 100% and made a mental note to sip white wine when grading my next batch of papers.

"Roses are red, and so is wine;

refill my glass, and I'll be fine."

WORDS FROM THE NOT SO WISE

BY T. EM EYE

As a drill team instructor at a high school I have a special relationship with my students and parents that can cause the lines of relationships to be blurred. Since we spend so much time together over multiple years, both the dancers and their parents will sometimes forget their filter when communicating with me. I had a parent tell me once that I was the devil because I didn't let her daughter dance in the front. Another time a young girl told me, "Mrs. Eye, I didn't send naked pictures. I was just on FaceTime when I was taking my clothes off." Perhaps one of the most disturbing conversations I've had with a student was about wearing bloomers under her costume. Her argument was, "If I wear bloomers how will boys know this is open for business?" Choreographing routines and taking home championship trophies doesn't even scratch the surface of what I deal with on a daily basis. I mean, really, sometimes there are just no words to effectively articulate what a teacher tackles at any given time.

"Every box of raisins is a tragic tale of grapes that could have been wine."

THANK YOU!

A NOTE OF THANKS TO WINEMAKERS

Dear Winemakers,

As a note of thanks, we raise our glasses at the end of each day in adoration and appreciation to you and your products. We know that without you our jobs of shaping the future would not hold the same joys. Whether we are reaching out to you for assistance in reducing stressors with a Pinot Noir or Merlot, washing away memories with a Zinfandel, or celebrating all the moments that remind us of the reasons we chose education as our profession in the first place with a Chardonnay; we know we couldn't do it without you. Thank you for your loyalty, reliability, and allegiance. Because of you, we are better teachers. Because of you we can combat conflict with grace when we are seeing red, we can stroke our egos after experiences that leave us blushing, and we can celebrate times the white light at the end of the tunnel is not actually a train. We would not stay true to ourselves if we didn't give you a little something in return. We spend hours every day influencing young minds. We would like to offer the same service to you now.

When whipping up your next blend of fermented grapes and seeking the perfect label, consider the following names:

Creative Juices

Not It

Weather Days

Inside Recess

Team Builder

Behavior Plan

Teacher's Pet

Summers Off

We wish you well and guarantee we will be seeing you soon.

Salut,

Educators

TEACHER'S CHOICE WINE LIST

Conundrum
www.conundrumwines.com

A to Z
www.atozwineworks.com

Greater than One
www.greaterthanonewines.com

1,000 Stories
www.1000storieswines.com

Chalkboard
www.chalkboardvineyards.com

Acronym
www.acronymwines.com

Las Niñas
www.vinalasninas.com

Educated Guess
www.rootsrundeep.com

Troublemaker
www.hopefamilywines.com

ACKNOWLEDGMENTS

Wine me up and watch me go! Pairing wines with scenarios and collecting true tales from teachers near and far has proven to be one of my favorite ventures. I could have never done it alone, so thank you to everyone who shared their tales so honestly and willingly with me. Your stories provide a portal into the lives of educators, allowing a tiny glimpse of what you face each and every day. They make a heart smile, a laugh snort, and at times a body cringe. They are truly unbelievable! As promised, I have changed names to protect the innocent. Your tales are safe with me. I wish you all well on your continued journeys in education. Just remember, whether your day has you feeling the glass is half empty, or half full, there is still more room for wine!